THE CHICA
ARCHITECTURE
BUILDING THE MODERN CITY, 1880-1910

Rolf Achilles

SHIRE PUBLICATIONS

MW01006799

Published in Great Britain in 2013 by Shire Publications Ltd, Midland House, West Way, Botley, Oxford OX2 0PH, United Kingdom.

43-01 21st Street, Suite 220B, Long Island City, NY 11101, USA.

E-mail: shire@shirebooks.co.uk   www.shirebooks.co.uk

A CIP catalog record for this book is available from the British Library.

Shire Library no. 741.   ISBN-13: 978 0 74781 239 5

Rolf Achilles has asserted his right under the Copyright, Designs and Patents Act, 1988, to be identified as the author of this book.

Designed by Tony Truscott Designs, Sussex, UK and typeset in Perpetua and Gill Sans.

Printed in China through Worldprint Ltd.

13 14 15 16 17   10 9 8 7 6 5 4 3 2 1

COVER IMAGE
The Reliance Building, 32 North State Street. (Library of Congress)

TITLE PAGE IMAGE
The Old Colony Building is in a row of other fine buildings on South Dearborn Street.

CONTENTS PAGE IMAGE
Stained glass designed by Sullivan, fabricated by Healy & Millet in Ganz Hall, inside the Auditorium Building.

ACKNOWLEDGEMENTS
This book is the result of listening to many remarkable people over several decades, artists, architects, engineers, historians, preservationists, and cultural critics all of them fascinated by what Chicago was and how it became what it is today. Special thanks to Tim Samuelson, The School of the Art Institute, Art History, Theory and Criticism Department and the Historic Preservation Department, Landmarks Illinois, Richard and Inese Driehaus, and Maral Hashemi.

PHOTOGRAPH ACKNOWLEDGEMENTS
From Rand McNally *Bird's Eye Views and Guide to Chicago*, 1898, Collection Tim Samuelson, pages 10, 22 (top); from *Prominent Buildings Erected by the George A. Fuller Company*, 1894, Collection Tim Samuelson, page 40 (top); from *Ornamental Iron*, Winslow Brothers Company, 1894, Collection Tim Samuelson, pages 7 (bottom), 40 (botom); from "Prominent Buildings Erected by the George A. Fuller Company," 1904. Collection Tim Samuelson, page 46 (top); from *Engineering News*, Dec. 21,1893. Collection Tim Samuelson, page 50 (top); postcard 5319, by Detroit Photographic Co., 1900, collection Tim Samuelson, page 55 (left). All other photographs by Rolf Achilles.

Shire Publications is supporting the Woodland Trust, the UK's leading woodland conservation charity, by funding the dedication of trees.

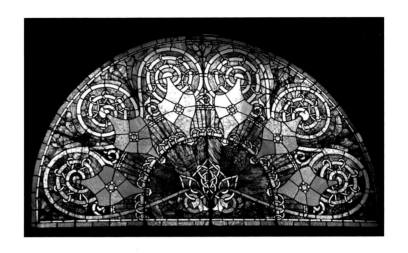

CONTENTS

INTRODUCTION   4

AFTER THE GREAT FIRE—FIREPROOFING   8

FOUNDATIONS SET IN WET SAND   14

TALL BUILDINGS   20

THERE'S A LIMIT TO HOW HIGH THE SKY   44

PLACES TO VISIT   63

FURTHER READING   63

INDEX   64

INTRODUCTION

IN ITS FIRST SEVENTY YEARS, Chicago was the fastest growing city the world had ever seen, with its population burgeoning from some three hundred people to 1.5 million between 1833 and 1900. Grappling with this unprecedented expansion, the city built to its horizons and its sky with machine-made iron and steel, bricks, terra-cotta, glass, cement, and all other materials demanded by a permanent boomtown that was contemporary by its own definition. Though only ten, eleven, and twelve stories high, the first steel-framed structures were taller than anything yet built. They seemed to go on forever, scraping the sky.

After the construction surge was over and some of the earliest buildings had already given way to new structures, historians had time to reflect on the recent past, calling what had happened the Commercial Style or Chicago School. Symbolizing civic unity and pride, the public's aspirations of upward mobility, these buildings were awe-inspiring. Their architects were among the first in the world to implement the new British and French technologies of steel-frame construction in commercial buildings. They have easily discernible unifying characteristics: a steel-frame with terra-cotta, brick or masonry cladding; a curtain wall of unlimited ornamentation pierced for large plate-glass windows; and an inner, private court for light and air, elevators, and more decoration.

As the nation's buildings began to multiply dramatically and grow ever bolder in their construction and use of materials, Barr Ferree spoke to the American Institute of Architects in 1893, telling them "current American architecture is not a matter of art, but of business. A building must pay or there will be no investor ready with the money to meet its cost." Not all were in agreement with this bold statement that buildings were strictly commercial ventures with little or no social responsibilities. Three years later Louis Sullivan penned his now famous lyrical essay in which he poetically argues that a tall building should be more than just functional, that it should be as beautiful as a tree, as stately as an ancient column, and most of all that its "form should ever follow" its function.

Opposite: Auditorium Tower by Adler & Sullivan, 1889. Briefly Chicago's tallest tower, the building was designed as a palace for people.

5

A typical Chicago curtain wall designed by Louis Sullivan in 1900 for Schlesinger & Mayer, since 1904 known as the Carson Pirie Scott department store.

All agreed that tall buildings were built from the inside out, that elevators were the internal determinant, but it was the outside—the building skin—that everyone saw. And it was the skin that made all the difference.

Knowing full well that tall buildings were built around elevators, Sullivan pleaded for art and natural beauty in tall structures to uplift the minds of those seeing them, while Ferree saw no ideal, just a straightforward approach to architecture that boldly reflected the cultural milieu of Chicago,

a chaotic Midwestern cosmopolis that was proud, western and nationalistic while exalting such nebulous ideals as "American" and "democracy." All that and much more was accomplished by the First Chicago School of Architecture. Today, Ferree is forgotten, his message taken to heart. Sullivan is now acclaimed as the developer of a Chicago style that became European Modernism and then returned to Chicago as the Second Chicago School led by German architect Ludwig Mies van der Rohe. Variants of the style are still very much active today across the world.

Above: The building of Burnham & Root's Fisher Building set a construction speed record.

Left: A steel-frame structure as it might have looked in the 1890s.

7

AFTER THE GREAT FIRE—FIREPROOFING

Built on sand and mud, Chicago developed from a messy mélange of humans and animals into a grid system for its streets; grain, lumber and animals for commerce; and a harbor on a slow-flowing two-branched river that also served factories and was used for sewage disposal, all the while flowing into an ocean-sized lake from which the city drank. It's an exciting story of human will over nature that differentiates Chicago from other cities.

In 1833, a small gathering of motley cabins, huts, and temporary shelters near a fort named Dearborn (indications of its foundations are well below today's intersection of East Wacker Drive and North Michigan Avenue) were perched on slightly elevated dry patches along the south bank of an almost stagnant river. Four years later, with just over four thousand inhabitants, Chicago was incorporated as a city. It boasted a courthouse, several churches and substantial homes, a bookstore, a theatre, a newspaper, three debating societies, a candy shop and the beginnings of a medical school.

By the 1850s, Irish, German, Italian, and Swedish immigrants, and New-England-born Americans were flooding to the city. The fact that the new city's ground was just inches above Lake Michigan's natural water table meant that the streets were mostly muddy, and there was not enough elevation for drainage to flow into the city's main sewer, the ever-stale Chicago River. The solution was to raise the central city's buildings some 6 or more feet. Work started in January 1858 on the northeast corner of Randolph Street when a 70-foot long, four-story, 750-ton brick structure was lifted by 200 jackscrews to a new grade level 6 feet 2 inches above the old—without "the slightest injury to the building," as the *Chicago Daily Tribune* reported. Some fifty similar-sized brick buildings quickly followed. Even an iron building weighing an estimated 27,000 tons, along with 230 feet of attached stone sidewalk, was lifted 27 inches. Less worthy wooden structures, sometimes even joined rows, were simply moved on rollers. While the technology was not new, its use on such a large scale was astounding to all who saw it and the world that read about it. It would not be the only time Chicago exploited technology; in fact, the whole of the ballooning city would continue to revel in its dependence on it.

Opposite:
Today noted for its innovative foundation, the Washington Block, built in 1873–4, is one of the earliest post-Great Fire buildings remaining in the Loop.

Map of downtown
Chicago in the
1890s. Black
rectangles are
railroad stations.

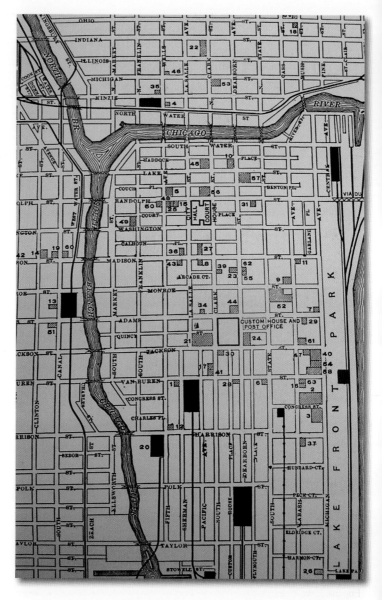

Then, after a wet spring in 1871, only 3¾ inches of rain fell between July 5 and October 8, the driest period in the recorded history of the city. The dryness resulted in a summer of many neighborhood fires, until the warm, windy, and dusty-dry evening of October 8, when the Great Chicago Fire ignited. Pushed by 20–40 mph winds, the flames rapidly spread from southwest to northeast through the downtown and many neighborhoods. When the fire finally died out on the morning of October 10, some 17,500 buildings were damaged or destroyed, leaving more than 100,000 homeless. Immediately the city began to rebuild. Employing newly invented technologies such as freeze-resistant mortar to set bricks, arc lamps for warmth and night construction under tarps, and mandating bricks over wood and iron within the city limits, Chicago began to rise from its ashes.

At first construction was hasty and followed tradition and fashionable wood and brick styles. But within a decade, commercial construction in the city's downtown became ever more innovative, systematically deploying state-of-the-art technology that allowed the construction of ever taller buildings. Traditional horizontal construction was quickly transformed by these new vertical machines that were devised for the sole purpose of enhancing production, were efficient to build and easy to use. Again, many of the innovations had been developed elsewhere, but their inspired use became distinctly Chicago's and brought about the Chicago School of Architecture in the 1880s and 1890s, lasting through to the 1910s.

But Chicago's first great wave of building was not solely the result of the Great Fire; it was also inspired by architectural innovation elsewhere in the world. Its immediate ancestor can be traced to late 1853, when Victor Baltard designed Paris's first truly freestanding iron structure, the Central Market at Les Halles. Les Halles consisted of cast-iron columns connected to roof trusses. The columns supported themselves and a roof of sheets of glass without masonry assistance. Floors were, in part, made of hollow clay tiles. Easy to clean and with very little structure to burn easily, the building was thought fireproof. Not everyone appreciated these innovations, with criticism coming from supporters of masonry. Even noted architect Eugene-Emmanuel Viollet-le-Duc—later a champion of iron construction— criticized Louis-Auguste Boileau's use of iron, claiming that changes in temperature could result in a "hail of bolt-heads, and during rain, a shower of rust."

In New York, architect and inventor James Bogardus (1800–74) designed and built a skeletal 175-foot tall eight-sided iron framework tower for the

The Great Chicago Fire of 1871 was one of several that followed an exceptionally dry summer.

McCullough Shot and Lead Company of New York City in 1855. The building was a success. Others followed in New York and elsewhere.

In Liverpool, Peter Ellis, Jr. designed an iron and glass structure in 1864 known as Oriel Chambers. Iron and glass bay windows make up its two exposed façades and the inner courtyard was faced with cantilevered iron cladding. Interestingly, John Wellborn Root was a teenager living in Liverpool at the time. Aspects of the Chicago Rookery he built with Daniel Burnham some two decades later may very well have been inspired by the Oriel Chambers.

The French, British and American ideas of fireproofing with iron construction, terra-cotta tiles and glass gained traction in France and Britain and were probably brought to Chicago first by George H. Johnson, master builder of fireproof grain-elevators, who had patented a system of hollow clay tiles for flooring, similar to ones he had seen in France early in 1871.

In Chicago, Johnson associated with John M. van Osdel, who was considered Chicago's first architect, and whom Johnson had worked for in the later 1860s. Van Osdel was working on a building at 40 North Dearborn Street that needed fireproofing of the kind Johnson specialized in. The foundation and walls of the Kendall Building had been built when the Great Chicago Fire temporarily halted construction. Construction continued immediately after the fire, but technical limitations of fire fighting and the problems associated with fire in recently invented elevator shafts restricted its height to five stories, one short of the planned six stories—which would have made it the city's tallest building. Johnson and the manufacturer claimed the system to be completely fireproof; however, the identity of the manufacturer of Johnson's patented tiles for the Kendall Building remains a mystery. Speculation points to the recently organized Chicago Terra-cotta Company. Directed by architect Sanford Loring and based on British technology, Chicago Terra-cotta had the capacity and at the time it was acclaimed as the leading manufacturer of terra-cotta in the US. Possibly because they were expensive, Johnson's hollow tiles never caught on.

While in theory, iron allowed for seemingly endless construction upward, Chicago's architectural efforts were restricted to a height of five stories for at least the next decade by its politicians' fear of fire and by available technology to prevent it. Meanwhile, New York, unrestrained by such concerns, continued apace to construct tall buildings.

It also did not help that Chicago was affected by the souring of the nation's economy after the September Panic of 1873, followed by what may have been a severe recession, if not depression. At the same time, the insurance companies that had willingly paid out for the Great Fire of 1871 had also loaned large sums for Chicago's reconstruction; sums that—due to the Panic of 1873—were now being defaulted on in unsustainable numbers. In addition, the tinder-quality construction that had led to the Great Fire still existed in

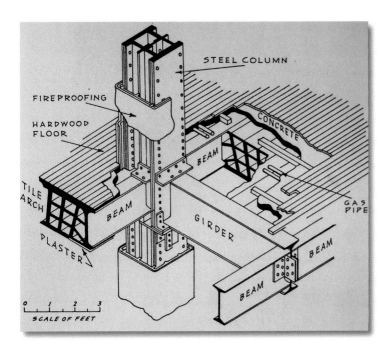

STEEL COLUMN

FIREPROOFING

HARDWOOD FLOOR

CONCRETE

BEAM

TILE ARCH

BEAM

PLASTER

GIRDER

GAS PIPE

BEAM

BEAM

0 1 2 3

SCALE OF FEET

William Le Baron Jenny's Fair Store, 1890–91, showing isometric detail of typical column-and-beam joint with Chicago fireproofing, advancing English and French developments.

Masonry skin cloaking a steel support was the ideal fireproofing solution at the time.

FIRE-PROOF BLOCKS

PLASTERING

the unburned South Side, at least until July 16, 1874, when 47 acres of it went up in flames. The flames quickly took in an area bounded by Clark, Polk, Michigan and Van Buren streets, stopping at the new masonry construction of Chicago's downtown—known as the Loop. This second fire burdened the insurance companies even more, to the point that The National Board of Underwriters petitioned the city council to enact reforms in construction, or the underwriters would have all existing fire policies cancelled.

Both the Great Fire of 1871 and the Fire of 1874 showed that cast iron was not fireproof. One of the reforms that the insurance companies wanted enacted was a ban of all cast-iron supports in favor of heavy wooden ones. If the insurance companies had their way, architectural cast-iron business would be over, at least in Chicago, meaning tall buildings could not be built and so ending Chicago's competition with New York. Something had to be done and quickly. It was in Chicago that Peter B. Wight, an architect, and Sanford Loring proved that their iron supports clad in fire-clay bricks would continue to support an exterior masonry skin even in great heat or when doused with water. In 1874, Wight patented the process. With the nation's economic recovery after the 1873 crash, Wight's process survived a series of lawsuits and became the favored Chicago way of fireproofing a building. This solution became Chicago's singular contribution to tall building construction.

FOUNDATIONS SET
IN WET SAND

WITH FIREPROOFING somewhat mastered, and Chicago having become something of a dry-topsoil city with the help of jacks and infill, large buildings were always a risk in the city's actual sandy, damp, often wet soil below the infill. Foundations built for the Washington Block, corner of North Wells and West Washington, in 1873–4 are a good example of how early builders of tall buildings tried to stabilize them in the city's moist soil. Built by brothers Frederick and Edward Baumann, at five stories it was one of Chicago's tallest buildings at the time.

To reach this height above the city's sandy, wet soil, Frederick Baumann invented a new support system. An isolated pier, acting much like later-developed pylons, was placed on its own foundation at each load-bearing point of the building to become a specific foundation segment. Walls were

New-Gothic-inspired window ornamentation on the Washington Block.

filled in between as needed. With this technique, any settling would be localized, isolated, and of little risk to the other supports. It worked, giving Chicago a cost-effective solution to erecting tall buildings in a swamp without compromising the building. For a decade or so, Baumann's isolated-pier foundation was a Chicago favorite.

William Le Baron Jenny (1832–1907), a Chicago-based engineer and architect, designed the Home Insurance Building in early 1884 and completed it in 1885. At the time, not much was said about it, but

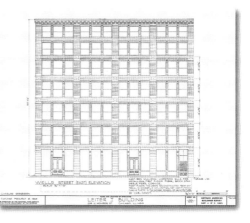

Jenny's Home Insurance Building is acclaimed as the first iron-framed tall office building in the United States.

a few years later it would be correctly claimed as the first iron-framed tall office building in the nation—and indeed the world. Building in iron, masonry and brick were not invented in Chicago, but the way they were assembled was.

Jenny received his formal education at Phillips Academy in Andover, Massachusetts and then at Harvard's Lawrence Scientific School. Seven years later, in 1853, Jenny went to Paris, to l'École Central des Arts et Manufactures to study engineering and architecture. He graduated in 1856, one year ahead of Gustave Eiffel, an engineering genius who would have a profound influence on him when it came to designing the Home Insurance Building. Jenny remained in Paris for several more years, during what was an exceptionally fertile time for French iron construction, only returning to the United States in 1861. Changes in the Paris construction code led directly to Eiffel's use of his technological advancement for the addition of a free-standing five-story wrought-iron framework inside the Grands Magasins du Bon Marché in the heart of Paris. The construction world was astounded and inspired.

Capitalizing on aspects of the new French technology, a grand department store—in both size and effect—was built in Cincinnati by dry-goods merchant John Shillito. Designed by James McLaughlin, the building's interior iron-skeleton frame and exterior masonry piers were configured in such a way to allow the interior to be free of load-bearing walls.

Not to be outdone by Cincinnati—a city which Chicago had long tussled with in meat packing and furniture manufacturing—Chicago's Marshall Field and Levi Leiter commissioned Jenny in 1879 to design a five-story warehouse for the northwest corner of Wells and Monroe streets. Today known as the First Leiter Building, it is generally acknowledged as the first Chicago School building. It was demolished in 1972. With its slender, widely spaced piers and spandrels, it was almost a copy of McLaughlin's Cincinnati design.

Jenny innovated on a French technique to open up the wall to windows as if it were a glass box. This building is generally thought of as the first Chicago School Building.

Three windows, each almost floor to ceiling, filled large rectangular areas. Bricks surrounded by cast-iron mullions framed the windows. The remaining walls served no weight-lifting function. These windows are the direct predecessors of what by the mid-1880s came to be called the "Chicago window." In the First Leiter, Jenny used the French technique of placing the iron pilaster on the inside of the masonry piers on the Wells Street side to support its timber floor-girders. This sleight of hand feature rendered the masonry piers unnecessary for carrying any floor loads. It also allowed them to be thinner, maximizing window size for more light. The resulting façade, though small, appeared as one large unit—almost making the building a glass box—something of a commercial kin to Sainte Chapelle, Paris.

Frank A. Randall noted in 1949, "had the wall columns been inserted in the piers, and had three more columns been added, the construction would have been essentially skeleton construction." Clever as First Leiter was, Jenny seems not to have taken a real step beyond the French system.

He would not take this step until 1884, in his Home Insurance Building, on the northeast corner of LaSalle and Adams, and then only on two façades facing the street. The other two remained traditional load-bearing brick walls. Jenny's overall design employing bolted and clamped iron elements was not a fully rigid load-bearing iron skeletal system as is often claimed, but a mix of the old, tried, and the new, untried, all in an effort to maximize the available light through large window openings. Light and air ventilation were necessary to make tall buildings functional and efficient, and most important, to sell interior space. To brighten interiors Edison's recently invented lightbulb was a step better than traditional gas, and certainly safer and cooler burning, but at around sixty watts, lighting was not sufficient to make the new sky-high stack of interiors functional and efficient work spaces without

At ten stories, the Home Insurance Building was a very early example of lightweight tall construction.

large windows. At 138 feet high, the Home Insurance Building stood ten stories tall and had a weight of about one-third that of an all-masonry building of equivalent height and mass. The Home Insurance building was demolished in 1931 to make room for the 535-foot forty-five-story tall Field Building, which has been called the Bank of America Building since 2007.

In 1891, Jenny was commissioned to design another building for Leiter, known as the Second Leiter Building, and later the Sears Building. It occupies the entire block along South State Street between East Van Buren and East Congress Parkway. At eight floors, each some 50,000 square feet, it is not particularly tall, but massive in its proportions. Faced with pink granite,

The Second Leiter
Building by Jenny,
1891, measures
400 feet along
State Street, and
as Siegel, Cooper
department store
became known as
the "Big Store."

Sober
ornamentation
helps emphasize
windows in Jenny's
design for the
Second Leiter
Building.

each of its nine grid-like bays facing State Street expresses the interior steel frame and is separated by wide pilasters with simple wide-leafed capitals. The north and south façades, measuring 400 feet by 143 feet, are three bays wide, with each bay having eight narrow or four wide sash windows. While owned by Levi Leiter, it was leased to Siegel, Cooper and Company department store for seven years. Claiming to be the largest retail floor area in the world, Siegel, Cooper called itself simply "Big Store." Jenny's unobstructed floor area certainly made it appear so. The building then went through various tenants before it became the flagship store of Sears, Roebuck & Co. from 1932 until 1986. Designated a Chicago landmark in 1997, it became the Chicago campus of Robert Morris University the following year.

Just up the street, at 126–144 South State, along Adams to Dearborn, the Fair Store was designed by Jenny and his then partner Mundy in 1892. Founded in Chicago in 1874 by Ernst J. Lehmann, the Fair billed itself as a discount department store and offered many different things for sale at odd prices, rather than at the customary multiple of 5 cents, saving the customer pennies on each purchase. Constructed much like the First Leiter building, the Fair was criticized for its gaudy ornament: heavy, huge capitals on the piers, a weighty cornice, all in an unforgiving salmon-toned terra-cotta, the whole considered a profusion of tasteless ornament which did not stop the Fair store from claiming to be the "largest mercantile establishment in the world." In 1896, the *Economist* claimed that it was even larger than Bon Marché of Paris. The Fair was purchased by Montgomery Ward in 1957, becoming its State Street flagship in 1963. It was sold and demolished in 1984.

William Le Baron Jenny's Fair Store, 1890–91.

TALL BUILDINGS

BEFORE Jenny's Home Insurance Building reached for the sky, others in Chicago were also striving for height. One such venture was the Montauk Building—also known as Montauk Block—designed by the architectural team of Burnham & Root (Daniel Burnham, 1846–1912, and John Wellborn Root, 1850–91). Built in 1882–3, the Montauk Block was demolished just twenty years later, in 1902, but not before Thomas Talmage, the famed Brooklyn clergyman, could praise, "What Chartres was to the Gothic cathedral, the Montauk Block was to the high commercial building." And, if Erik Larson, author of *Devil and the White City*, is correct, the Montauk is the first building called a "Skyscraper." At 115 Monroe Street, on a frontage of 90 feet with a depth of 180 feet, the Montauk stood 130 feet tall, counted ten stories, and boasted 150 offices for 300 occupants. Two elevators provided service to the upper floors. After the Montauk was demolished, the First National Bank was built on its site, 1903–6, which in turn was demolished in 1965 to create the First National Bank and Plaza, now the Chase-Morgan Bank and Plaza.

Of the Montauk and other Root-designed buildings, architectural historian Carl Condit writes in his monumental *The Chicago School of Architecture*,

> It was John Wellborn Root who led the way in bringing the building art of the nineteenth century to its maturity. It was Root who took the ultimate step of freeing the big commercial building from any dependence on masonry adjuncts and creating the plan and structure of the urban office block as we know it today!

That may be so, but Root, until his death from influenza in 1891, found much inspiration around him in Chicago.

Just before the "ultimate step" described by Condit, Burnham & Root designed the Rookery in 1887. Completed in 1888, the Rookery still stands on the southeast corner of the West Adams at 209 South LaSalle. Measuring 181 feet tall, twelve stories, the Rookery is the oldest high-rise standing in Chicago. At one time the offices of Burnham & Root were on its top floor.

Opposite:
The Reliance Building shows how by 1894 Burnham & Root had reduced the façade to a skeleton, a "beinahe nichts" (almost nothing) as Mies van der Rohe would call it a few decades later.

21

Rookery Building, bird's-eye view looking south from Adams and LaSalle, c. 1898.

Below: Coining the descriptive word "skyscraper," the Montauk (no.8) was much more influential than its twenty-year lifespan would suggest. No.9 is the First National Bank Building, no.10 is the Stock Exchange Building, no.4 is the Fair Store.

The Rookery's internal steel frame is in keeping with the most current technology while its exterior load-bearing walls appear to be traditional granite, brick, terra-cotta, cast-iron and glass. This mix of old and new is one of transition. Eventually the visual hybrid of the Rookery gave way to an economy of fire-resistant materials aesthetically cloaking the skeletal steel frame that became universally accepted for tall structures.

Burnham & Root's
Rookery Building,
view from LaSalle
and Quincy
streets, is
the world's
oldest standing
iron-framed
"skyscraper."

One important architectural innovation did set the Rookery apart from its contemporaries: the use of a reinforced-concrete slab that in effect "floated" on the city's soft, swampy belly. Also called a grillage foundation, it was a crisscross of iron rails and structural beams encased into a concrete slab thick enough to support the full weight of the building that rose on it.

Like St. Christopher carrying his burden, the floating slab became ever more supportive as the building gained height, its weight forcing

The Rookery takes its name from the John Holabird Root-designed cackling birds on the pink granite spring stones of the main entrance arch.

Elaborate and innovative red Chicago-made terra-cotta ornaments are proportionately distributed on the Rookery's façades.

water out of the moist Chicago soil until the whole of the foundation was stable enough to support the completed building. This technique eliminated traditional, heavy individual piers, or building stones, each of which settled at its own pace, thus weakening itself and unbalancing what it supported. Traditionally a mason used his skills and experience to judge that the weight distribution was uniform enough to press evenly across all the foundation stones as the height of the building increased, a tradition fine for dry soils and relatively low buildings. In Chicago engineering supported by science and technology converted the damp soil to solid foundations.

A fine, granulated red granite worked in three distinct techniques—rustic, dressed, and polished—gave the pedestrian a reassuring façade along Adams and LaSalle. Stacked bay windows flooded the ground-floor shop with natural light, showing products as clearly as if they were on the sidewalk. A few years later this display technique would be fully exploited on State Street. This was a tradition in the making.

The massive two-story ground-floor façade is pierced by two entrances, a secondary one facing Adams and a primary one of huge rusticated blocks and finely dressed ornament which would promote strength and ancient stability if it were not for the whimsy of eye-level left and right high-relief capitals depicting squabbling birds designed by Root, hence "Rookery."

This is Root's take on Richardsonian Romanesque, an American aesthetic developed by Henry Hobson Richardson in Boston with recently completed key Chicago exponents, the Marshall Field's warehouse, downtown, and the Glessner House, Prairie Avenue at 18th Street.

Above the massive entrance, half-round columns reach for the cornice, separating sets of windows stacked five high into ribbons that encircle the building. Ornamental terra-cotta spandrels tether the columns and decorate the underside of the balcony. Just under the cornice a ribbon of window allows maximum light into these upper offices, once those of Burnham & Root.

Today called a doughnut-shaped building, the inside central light-court with its twelve floors of white glazed bricks and reflective gold leaf ornament was highly innovative in 1887 for allowing almost the same amount of light inside offices as do the windows of the exterior offices. The interior-court ceiling is a skylight covered in ornamental ironwork and glass with its own small movable windows to enhance air circulation. All around the inner court large windows allow light into the shops facing the court. Above these windows is a metal-grid walkway paved with glass squares admitting a faint glow to penetrate the shops from above. At a time when the electric bulb was still a controversial alternative to gas, every surface in the Rookery's courtyard was designed to let in natural light.

In 1905, when the Rookery was almost twenty years old, Frank Lloyd Wright was hired to update its interior. He cloaked much of the dark ornate

The Rookery Court façade retains some of its original Luxfer prism glazing.

metal in fine white Carrara marble, which he "enhanced" with high-relief vines set against a gold leaf ground. Wright reconfigured the grand stair's supports and painted all but the stair metal and balustrade a creamy white in keeping with the glazed bricks of the inner court walls. Wright also designed hanging lights using Luxfer's newest prismatic bulb covers. In 1931, William Drummond, a former Wright assistant, again modernized the interior, including new elevators and light fixtures. The building hit hard financial times in the 1950s and it was not until the early 1990s that another restoration and a general repair occurred. In 2007 a full restoration was undertaken.

Outside along Quincy Street and continuing around the corner along Rookery Court to Adams, large double windows set in cast-iron frames are the ground-floor façade. This is the first glass curtain wall of its kind in a tall building in Chicago and in the United States. The skinny vertical supports holding the glass also appear to be holding up the upper dozen floors of brick. They do not. The cast iron columns are holding themselves and the glass, while the inside steel frame is holding up most everything else.

In his *History of the Development of Building Construction in Chicago*, John A. Randall quotes Edward A. Renwick as writing,

The Rookery's atrium balcony retains its original glass flooring. Considered innovative today, glass floors were common in tall buildings when there were only dim alternatives to natural light.

The Rookery's light-court maximizes natural light on the building's interior. Most of the original dark bronze and iron interior was rendered white in Frank Lloyd Wright's interior renovations in 1906–7. Wright also designed the dark light fixtures.

The Rookery's Quincy Street glass and cast-iron façade appears to hold up the wall above it.

The conical bend of the Monadnock's corner gives it a dramatic sweep.

When Owen Aldis put up the Monadnock on Jackson boulevard there was nothing on the south side of the street between State street and the river but cheap one-story shacks, mere hovels. Everyone thought Mr. Aldis was insane to build way out there on the ragged edge of the city. Later when he carried the building on through to Van Buren Street they were sure he was.

The solid masonry construction of the Monadnock relies on bricks and visual illusions to appear ancient. The Monadnock's thick walls can be seen in the window placement. Only the bays have conventional flush window openings.

For the then "ragged edge of the city," Burnham & Root designed an unadorned slab, two bays wide and sixteen stories high (197 feet). Funded by Peter and Shepherd Brooks and Owen Aldis between 1889 and 1891, the Monadnock was and remains a radically different building than all the others of the First Chicago School. Upon completion the Monadnock was the world's largest office building. Randall also told his readers in 1949 that the Monadnock was the heaviest building built in Chicago.

Its narrowness allowed outside exposure for every office opening into a single corridor running down the central length of each floor. Where the Rookery was built—only a couple of years before—in a doughnut shape for internal light, the atrium of the Monadnock is more like a light shaft than a doughnut, and is filled with a single iron staircase rising the full sixteen floors of the building. The stair's ground-floor newel and stair-sides and baluster grills are of a new material, aluminum. Aluminum was also cast into light fixtures, mailboxes, and heating grates, resulting in the first ever large-scale use of aluminum inside a building. Yet it is the unadorned exterior that inspired awe—sixteen stories of brick, not a brick facing, but solid through and through, more than 6 feet thick at the base. Massive, dressed red-granite blocks support lintels across the entrances. Below grade

The Monadnock's addition is a steel-frame structure with a curtain-wall of brick and terra-cotta, rather than the solid masonry and granite of the original. Its construction was also more cost effective.

The Monadnock's ground-floor newel and balusters, mailboxes and light fixtures are the first large-scale use anywhere of aluminum inside a building.

The Monadnocks' aluminum light fixture is a Chicago version of Art Nouveau.

the granite giants stand on a great concrete and steel raft that extends some 11 feet out from the exterior walls of the building. The eventual weight of the building was calculated to sink the foundation by 8 inches. It finally sank it by some 20 inches, requiring a raising of the inner ground-level floor.

Inside the Monadnock's walls is a hidden frame of cast- and wrought-iron portions which are configured into a wind-bracing system that may be the first of its kind for an iron-frame structure. Jenny's Manhattan Building, a block away, is usually given credit for this important structural development, but it was designed at the same time as the Monadnock, so both developed simultaneously.

Harriet Moore, a poet and Root's sister-in-law, later wrote that the Monadnock had been an aesthetic struggle for Root:

> For this building, Mr. Aldis, who controlled the investment, kept urging upon the architects extreme simplicity, rejecting one or two of Root's

The original ferris wheel was designed and constructed by George Washington Gale Ferris, Jr. as the centerpiece of Chicago's 1893 World's Columbian Exhibition overseen by Daniel Burnham.

Night view of World's Columbian Exposition architecture, which Louis Sullivan said would set architecture back fifty years.

sketches as too ornate. During Root's absence of a fortnight at the seashore, Mr. Burnham ordered from one of the draftsmen a design of a straight-up-and-down, uncompromising, unornamented façade. When Root returned, he was indignant at first over this project of a brick box. Gradually, however, he threw himself into the spirit of the thing, and one day he told Mr. Aldis that the heavy sloping lines of an Egyptian pyramid had gotten into his mind as the basis of this design, and that he thought he would "throw the thing up without a single ornament." At last, with a gesture whose pretense of disgust concealed a shy experimental interest, he threw on the drawing table

Souvenir books and photograph albums of the 1893 World's Fair were published in several languages. This is a German one.

of Mr. Dutton, the foreman of the office, "a design," says this gentleman, "shaped something like a capital I—a perfectly plain building curving outward at base and cornice." This was the germ of the final design, and it provoked much study and discussion in the office.

While looking and acting like a skyscraper, at sixteen stories the Monadnock defined the limits of masonry construction and became the proof that this millennia-old tradition was not a solution for future skyscrapers.

At the time of the Monadnock's completion, *Carpentry and Building*, a New York-based magazine, wrote:

> The character of the structures erected demonstrates one notable fact—
> that is, that for the first time architects have risen to the plane of the highest
> constructive knowledge in structures… In this respect Chicago is unique,
> and it is a common remark in Eastern and foreign cities … that Chicago
> today erects the best building structures ever known, and with the notable
> distinction that she does it with the closest economy in materials and time.
> That is to say … in Chicago buildings the quality is better, the distribution
> of material is more skillful, and the buildings are naturally more reliable.

Root died of pneumonia in 1891, leaving Burnham to fend for himself through much of the design and construction of the 1893 Chicago World Columbian Exposition. Burnham was a quick study who kept up-to-date on the latest aesthetic fads and technical ideas, shifting his pitch as needed in order to generate sales. After his successful directorship of the Classical and Renaissance Revival look of the Exposition he quickly shed his innovative Chicago commercial style, the one that had made him famous, opting for more traditional elements and heavier façades that espoused new wealth over innovation and novelty. Louis Sullivan summed it up when he wrote, "The damage wrought by the World's Fair will last for half a century from its date."

Remaining structures of the First Chicago School give the impression of an organized progression. It was not originally thus. Around the time Adler & Sullivan's Auditorium Building was first announced, critics and pundits in Chicago spoke of what was happening. Echoing these discussions the *Chicago Tribune*, November 7, 1886, printed, "when Chicago takes old Rome's arches and sticks on top of them a skyscraper block containing 5,000 rooms, a café, an opera-house, a barber shop, a billiard saloon, the whole thing is an architectural triumph and justly belongs to the new school of Chicagoesque."

While Chicago was defining the skyscraper, another building with an office tower actually

Cartoonist John T. McCutcheon drew a series of cartoons capturing the frenzied building of Chicago.

THE FRENCH EMISSARY STUDIES OUR INDUSTRIAL METHODS

Adler & Sullivan's innovative Auditorium Building had an auditorium as well as a hotel, office complex, restaurants and shops. Today it is the home of Roosevelt University.

defined Chicago. This other building was the Auditorium Building, designed by Adler & Sullivan. Born in 1844 in Stadtlengsfeld, Thuringia, Germany, Dankmar Adler came to Chicago in 1866, set up his own firm in 1880, hired Louis Sullivan as a draftsman and then made him a partner in 1883, and died in 1900 in Chicago. Louis Sullivan was born in 1856 in South Reading, Massachusetts. He briefly studied architecture at the Massachusetts Institute of Technology, worked in Philadelphia for Frank Furness, then moved to Chicago in 1873. He died in Chicago in 1924.

In 1885, the firm of Adler & Sullivan won a commission—underwritten by Ferdinand W. Peck, an ardent supporter of the arts—to design an enormous multi-use auditorium complex to be called, simply, the Auditorium. By early 1887 overall plans were completed; construction started. Two years later the Auditorium opened to the public.

Auditorium
Theatre
Building interior
plasterwork by
Healy & Millet
and Decorators
Supply showing
typical Louis
Sullivan-inspired
acanthus leaves
being modern,
not classical.

At the time, the Auditorium was the most complex structure built in the United States. At ten stories high, with a tower extending to seventeen stories, its 63,350 square-foot plan covered the block along Congress Avenue between Michigan and Wabash. Serving as its name implies, as an auditorium, it housed a hotel, restaurants, and offices, and was the south anchor of Michigan Avenue.

Auditorium
Theatre mosaic
floor designed
by Louis Sullivan
and fabricated by
Healy & Millet.

35

The Auditorium's visible foundations are traditional load-bearing walls of solid masonry clad in rough-faced gray granite for the first three stories, limestone the next seven.

Before the widening of Congress Boulevard, the main Auditorium Theatre entrance was indicated by a tower, whose initial function was to hold the water tanks required in part by the hydraulic lifts of the stage. The tower was billed as the tallest building in Chicago until the plans released for the Monadnock Building, by Burnham & Root, showed their building to be intentionally one floor taller. Although several floors of the Auditorium's tower were already constructed, the Auditorium's board pressured Sullivan (Adler was in Budapest looking at stage machinery) without consulting Adler, to redesign it taller. Sullivan's tower added an extra 1,200 tons over the entrance, and caused the Auditorium's outer lobby to warp significantly, but it won the day, no doubt to the great surprise of the developers of the Monadnock.

Alluding to what lay inside, green copper stamped with Sullivan's ornaments was used to accent the door and window surrounds of the Michigan entrance. Variegated onyx wainscoting in the Michigan Avenue lobby and first stair-landing adds an abstract display uncommon in the 1880s, with its Japanism styling presaging Art Nouveau. Throughout the Auditorium acanthus foliage tops doorways, ribbons around rooms, capitals, and balusters. Scagliola resembling marble and other stone decorates columns and walls. Cast-plaster rosettes (fabricated by Decorators Supply, a Chicago firm that continues to thrive) studded with clear-glass, carbon-filament bulbs brighten the walls and ceilings to an amber glow.

Healy & Millet, a Chicago decorating and design juggernaut, fabricated the Auditorium's stained-glass windows and floor mosaics, as well as metalwork, wood carvings, murals and gilding after designs by Louis Sullivan. Healy & Millet were unmatched in the US and in Europe at the time. When Sullivan's designs from the Auditorium Building, as fabricated by Healy & Millet, were exhibited at the Paris World's Fair of 1889, they won a government purchase prize and remained in Paris on exhibit after the fair, eventually moving to the Musée D'Orsay where they remain on view. To this day, a tour of the Auditorium building gives a good idea of the work of Adler & Sullivan and Healy & Millet as it was seen by the world for the first time in 1889.

Seating 4,237 people, the Adler-designed Auditorium Theatre is the core of the structure. A vast, high-arched room with no conventional chandeliers, it featured only the newest technology—air-cooling through its enormous supporting

Auditorium Theatre, one of many examples of innovative stained glass fabricated by Healy & Millet based on Louis Sullivan designs. Healy & Millet exhibited Sullivan's designed glass for the Auditorium Theatre Building at the Paris World's Fair of 1889 and changed the way Europe saw stained glass.

Healy & Millet fabricated glass in the stairwell of the Auditorium Building, now Roosevelt University.

arches, variable adjustable interior spaces and a stage that could be elevated in sections, which lent the interior multiple uses. All the while, cool, clear glass bulbs washed each patron evenly in an amber glow. The great overhead arches made columns unnecessary, giving each seat a clear line of sight while Adler's superb engineering delivered perfect acoustics. Technically the Auditorium could do anything, except make money.

With the construction of the Union Loop elevated streetcar line, the Auditorium's offices facing Wabash Street became noisy and did not rent as expected. By 1906, Theodore Thomas and the Chicago Symphony moved from their original home in the Auditorium

Detail of Healy & Millet fabricated glass in the stairwell of the Auditorium Building.

Replications of Sullivan-designed electroliers in Ganz Hall inside the Auditorium Building, now a Roosevelt University music recital room.

to Symphony Hall, designed by Daniel Burnham. In 1946 Roosevelt College (now University) took over the complex, changing much of the interior into offices. Within a decade Congress Parkway was widened to accept the Eisenhower Expressway and the long bar inside the Auditorium Building made way for a sidewalk. More changes happened until the Auditorium became the venue for rock shows and Broadway spectacles—anything that paid the bills. It was not until the 1980s that the genius of Louis Sullivan and Dankmar Adler was again recognized and the Auditorium began to be cared for as one of the nation's most influential architectural monuments.

While the Auditorium became an immediate international sensation, Chicago architects explored other styles, seemingly not feeling an urge to nurture what the world took note of in the Auditorium. Nor apparently did Chicagoans have the leisure to theorize a movement. The result was a series of commercial buildings, each majestically important and trendsetting in its own way without being a unique force for its own aesthetic. This was not the case in Europe, where, once the Auditorium's decoration was exhibited in Paris, any number of architects and artists, such as Victor Horta or Henry van de Velde, championed the new look as a style of their own creation, a style that by 1900 was known in France and Belgium as Le Art Nouveau; in Germany as Jugendstil; and in England, Italy and throughout the Balkans as the Liberty Style.

Stained glass designed by Sullivan, and fabricated by Healy & Millet in the foyer ceiling of Ganz Hall.

With the Auditorium Building still new on the city skyline, the Tacoma Building by Holabird & Roche rose on the northeast corner of LaSalle and Madison in 1889. Because of its bold, new system of construction and rational and functional use of materials, the Tacoma would today be the poster-child of Chicago School buildings if it were still in existence. The Tacoma introduced several innovations, in particular its unique foundation. Before Holabird & Roche started to build, they initiated several 50-foot test borings that found water and soft clay. These deposits were emptied and the borings were then filled with concrete forced in under pressure. Then highly innovative, today this is a common practice. To stabilize the foundation, columns supporting the building were secured on floating rafts of concrete 20 inches thick, and reinforced with steel I-beams. Carl Seiffert was the inventive structural engineer. Cast iron, wrought iron and Bessemer steel made up the floor, roof, and wind-load supports of the Tacoma. Although it was long known that this construction was inspired engineering, it was not really understood how exemplary Holabird & Roche and Seiffert had been with the Tacoma Building until it gave way in 1929 to the One North La Salle Building by Vitzthum & Burns.

Tacoma Building,
built 1886–9.
Typical floor plan.

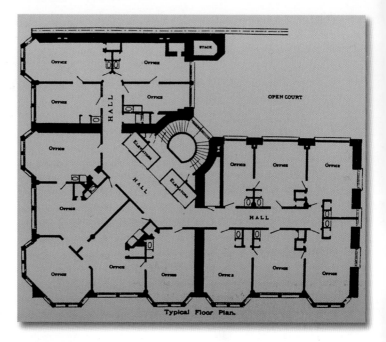

Typical Floor Plan.

Tacoma Building
1886–9. Typical
spandrel section.

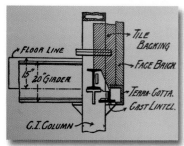

At 431 South Dearborn, a city block south of the Monadnock, the sixteen-story Manhattan Building was designed by William Le Baron Jenny and built between 1889 and 1891. Though probably the first structure to employ smaller upper stories—later called set-backs—today the Manhattan is acclaimed as the oldest surviving skyscraper in the world to use a skeletal support structure exclusively. A granite façade topped by one of bricks makes for a solid-looking yet sturdy structure that lightens the load on its internal steel frame as it goes up. Bay windows provide light for the interior and also help lighten the façade. The north and south walls are of brick and hollow tile, supported on steel cantilevers cleverly hooked back into the internal framework to lighten the load on the façade. Variations of this technology are still in use today.

Lightening the load, reducing visible materials to what Ludwig Mies van der Rohe would later call "beinahe nichts" (almost nothing), within four years of receiving the commission for alterations, Burnham & Root turned their proposal into a demolition and new construction. With plans completed by Charles Atwood in 1894, and structural engineering by Edward C. Shankland, the remarkable fourteen-story Reliance Building was occupied within a year.

Building in Chicago is often deservedly described in superlatives. The steel frame of the top ten stories of the Reliance was completed in fifteen days, remarkable speed given the available technical support in 1895. This steel system is different from others nearby. For wind bracing it consists of a series of 24-inch-deep spandrel girders with some clever supports that rigidly bolt the structural webbing securely to the two-story-long columns at staggered intervals. The resulting façade is almost not there, "beinahe nichts" in its series of vertical anorexic mullions interrupted by large expanses of glass—that looks as if it can't possibly hold itself up, a functioning nothing that is breathtaking. The dark horizontal ground floor sets the pace

Manhattan Building by William Le Baron Jenny is acclaimed as the oldest surviving steel-framed skyscraper anywhere and it is among the first buildings to diminish its upper stories, later called set-backs.

The Manhattan Building's bay windows lighten its load.

for the stack of horizontal slabs, each cloaked by an articulated band of creamy terra-cotta. The serious support system of columns and girders is inside, hidden from view. The large, single-paned sheets of glass flanked by a narrow movable sash are set nearly flush to their frames, giving them a skin quality that had not previously been achieved in Chicago windows. Atwood did not retreat from the airy, apparent nothingness of the façade, a nothingness that Ludwig Mies van der Rohe would take up again almost fifty years later, in 860–880 North Lake Shore Drive.

At the same time that the Loop was developing innovative ways to build tall buildings with steel frames, the recently organized Chicago firm of Beers, Clay and Dutton was building a steel-framed residence for William H. Reid at 2013 S. Prairie Avenue. Steel girders support its three metal-reinforced concrete floors, two of which are pierced by a great staircase and a central octagonal opening topped by a stained-glass dome. Some of the house's girders span the 25-foot width of the house. The Reid House still stands and is now considered the earliest surviving house built with a skyscraper-like steel frame. It has the other distinction of being the only house on Prairie Avenue that has always, since its construction in 1894, been a single-family residence.

While two façades are famously almost not there, very traditional brick walls cloak the two other walls of the Reliance Building.

Upon its completion in 1892, the Burnham & Root-designed Masonic Temple, on the northwest corner of Randolph and State, attracted special attention. At twenty-one stories it was tall—the tallest building in the world at the time. Its central court, a hollow core for all of its twenty-one stories, was topped by a skylight. The hollow core soon became a standard for tall

The Palladian-
inspired brick and
terra-cotta façade
hides the fact that
the Reid House
is built on a
steel frame.

The bar at the
top of the Masonic
Temple. When the
twenty-one-story-
tall Masonic
Temple was
completed it was
the tallest building
in the world.

buildings in Chicago and elsewhere. Like the Auditorium, it
was a mixed-use interior of which its first nine floors were
retail shops, above which followed twelve stories with some
five hundred offices, including rooms for the Masons. An
observation deck at 302 feet gave the public a fine panorama
of the lake and city. All this was supported by a rigid steel
frame and wrought-iron wind-bracing above the tenth floor.

THERE'S A LIMIT TO HOW HIGH THE SKY

WHEN THE Masonic Temple was completed, it was the tallest building in the city. It would remain so until the late 1920s, because its height immediately kindled memories of how technology and its machines had met their limits in the Great Fire. In reaction to the height and massiveness of the Masonic Temple, a city council ordinance of 1892 limited building heights to a maximum of 130 feet. Building height was limited to 125 feet on streets less than 80 feet wide and to 100 feet on streets less than 40 feet wide.

At city council meetings and in the press, various professionals, civic associations and others chimed in on the proper form and height of downtown buildings. The discussions brought up many points about the new buildings that architects and their supporters did not also trumpet. Critics insisted that investors, trying to win tenants and profits, should not be permitted to ignore the surrounding city. They pointed out that while a model of internal coordination, almost to a building the new construction manifested a disturbing degree of design anarchy in relation to the city plan and streetscape. The critics pointed out that what happens on the sidewalk is as important as what happens in the building, maybe even more so because it affects many more people.

The debate revolved around some apparent contradictions: with their metal frames, large windows, huge light-courts, and careful planning, skyscrapers promised light, airy, and healthy office accommodations. However, critics noted that the tall buildings were casting the city streets into shadow, making the air stagnant and thus threatening public health. Furthermore, the burning of one million tons of soft coal annually in Chicago for office buildings' heating, elevators, and lighting plants produced dark soot over the whole of the downtown, belying the promise of light and clean air made in skyscraper rental brochures. Skyscrapers promised an efficient concentration of business, which critics attacked for congesting streets and making downtown a less efficient place for business. While skyscrapers incorporated a number of innovations in fireproofing, critics noted that because of their height and the necessary elevator shafts, they rendered

Opposite:
Superb glass mosaics designed by A. J. Holzer with Tiffany-made Favril glass, depicting scenes from Marquette's visit to Chicago, line the atrium of the Marquette Building.

45

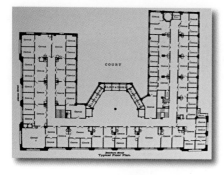

A typical floor plan of the Marquette Building.

traditional fire-fighting methods ineffective and increased the hazard of fires spreading to other parts of the city.

Skyscrapers, their builders and users insisted, represented a legitimate exercise of property rights. This, said the critics, was inflicting damage on the property of their neighbors.

Meanwhile, skyscrapers continued to be built and mostly applauded as developers and their architects countered cleverly by packaging their deeds as

The Marquette's steel frame inside clearly defines the façade outside. Alexander Calder's *Flamingo* shows a leg in the foreground.

ennobling commerce with monumental forms, using rich materials, traditional architectural motifs, state-of-the-art technology, cultivating white-collar aspirations and much more, all for the public good. After some forty years of striving towards the sky, architects had reformulated the image of commerce and its tall buildings, claiming it a natural American aspiration that the whole world admired.

In 1893, Peter Brooks, a Boston real-estate speculator, built the Marquette Building on the northwest corner of Adams and Dearborn, today, 140 South Dearborn. Brooks was no stranger to Chicago. With his brother Charles, he had most recently commissioned the steel-frame terra-cotta and brick-clad southern addition to the Monadnock from Holabird & Roche. For his new venture, Brooks again turned to Holabird & Roche. The Marquette is a sixteen-story, steel-framed structure engineered by Purdy and Handerson. The Marquette opened for occupancy in 1894. Today, carefully restored for the McArthur Foundation, the Marquette is arguably the defining First Chicago School building because it incorporates and radiates all the various technical and architectural nuances that made Chicago such an influential center of architecture in the 1880s and 1890s.

Its façade is ribbon upon ribbon of large Chicago windows separated by vigorous vertical and horizontal bands of dry-blood-colored terra-cotta and brick clearly indicating the underlying structure. Row upon row of large horizontal sheets of glass were cut from many enormous muffs mechanically blown in the facilities of Pittsburgh Plate Glass, Pittsburgh, Pennsylvania to create the windows. Each window is a single sheet or two of glass flanked by accompanying small sashes that together fill a whole bay. At the time, these were the largest sheets of glass the world had ever seen. These windows allow in maximum light with adequate ventilation left and right, all the while expressing fully the steel frame holding up everything.

The Marquette is an enormous "E" with its long elevation facing Dearborn, leaving the shorter central stem, the lobby, relatively dark. But this does not matter much because,

Between the steel supports of the Marquette Building, there was ample space for large windows, soon to be called the Chicago window, and later, picture window.

Glass for the Marquette Building mosaics came from Ottawa, Illinois.

unlike earlier buildings, the lobby functions solely as a six-sided perimeter for ten double-decked elevators. This elevator configuration, innovative at the time, consumes the same building space as a single elevator while doubling the shaft's capacity. Originally these were cage elevators that allowed exterior light into the cage and into the lobby.

Each elevator door was topped by a bronze head of either a local Native American tribal elder or a member of Jacques Marquette's 1673–74 expedition. Swiss artist A. J. Holzer created three scenes from Marquette's expedition, three dedicatory panels and six standing figures in superb Tiffany-fabricated Favril glass mosaics on the solid railing that surrounds the polygonal lobby. The mosaics have a unique luster that may be due to the quality of sand used to make the glass, pure quartz crystal from Ottawa, Illinois.

For the next decade Holabird & Roche continued to dilute the aesthetic theme they had started with the Marquette. The exception to this slow fade was their seventeen-story Old Colony Building, constructed in 1893–94. Engineered by Corydon T. Purdy as a mix of tried wrought-iron frame construction, and steel floor and girder beams, this highly innovative system of wind bracing created a rigid frame by means of girders, columns and bridge-like arch configurations. The Old Colony is rather narrow and open on all four sides with none of the masonry load-bearing walls that had traditionally provided rigidity. Four slab-like façades allow a maximum of natural light through Chicago-style windows on each end. Relatively small sash windows provide light for offices otherwise. Each corner has a rounded bay that seems to serve only an aesthetic consideration of making the narrow end wall with its Chicago windows appear wider and the wide wall with its smaller windows narrower.

Opposite: Holabird & Roche's Old Colony Building, built 1893–4.

While structurally employing a skeleton steel frame like a typical Chicago School commercial structure, the Brewster Apartments, originally known as the Lincoln Park Palace, northwest corner of Pine Grove and Diversey, is not easily overlooked with its exterior of massive rough-cut blocks of red

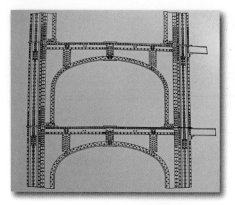

granite on all four sides, akin to Richardson's medieval ideals but much rougher and seemingly larger. It was designed by Enoch Hill Turnock, an otherwise unacclaimed architect who was born in England, grew up in Elkhart, Indiana, studied at the School of the Art Institute of Chicago and worked for several years in the Chicago offices of William Le Baron Jenny. The Brewster apartments were built in 1893, a year of great financial turmoil in much of the United States that mostly bypassed Chicago because of its World's Columbian Exposition.

Bridge-like arches are a unique wind-bracing structure in the Old Colony Building.

Cylindrical corners give the Old Colony great stability and a unique look among Chicago's early skyscrapers.

Opposite; Originally known as the Lincoln Park Palace, the Brewster is one of the very few early skyscraper apartment buildings to survive. It retains its original Louis Sullivan-inspired terra-cotta crown.

Today, the Brewster's overall construction and apartment layout is like a very old hotel that does not prepare you for its original and bold interior plan that maximizes light through its hollow, rectangular eight-story atrium interior capped by a skylight. The atrium contains a cage elevator, pierced iron stairs, railings and glazed "skywalks" that hang, bridge-like, the length of the atrium with short spurs to each apartment along its width. The translucent flooring is a grid of 4x4 inch square glass bricks set in an iron frame. To maximize available light to the interior of each apartment, windows pierce the interior atrium's brick walls as well as the exterior walls. The Brewster's interior, already fully electrified in 1893, is a rare reminder of the marvelous few years when the lightbulb was young and natural light still dominated. While briefly employed by Chicago's Essanay Studios in 1915–6, Charlie Chaplin lived in the Brewster's penthouse.

The Brewster is a steel-framed building with granite cladding on all four façades.

Enoch Turnock combines several Chicago School features such as bays and cylindrical corners on his Brewster building.

Solon S. Beman, born in Brooklyn, New York in 1853, died in Chicago, 1914, studied with Richard Upjohn and then came to Chicago in 1879, where he quickly found success. Among his many accomplishments was the design of the nation's first planned company town, Pullman; the eclectic Studebaker Building (1884–5), today the Fine Arts Building, 410 South Michigan; and less well known, the ten-story Studebaker Building at 623 S. Wabash. Originally built in 1895 for the Studebaker Brothers Carriage Company of South Bend, Indiana, as its Chicago regional office and warehouse, the west-facing façade is all glass supported by a subordinated tracery of Gothic-inspired elements. It is an early glass curtain wall. The horizontal spandrels are structural iron plates exposed as façade elements. In total, this façade is one of the finest examples of how steel and glass were combined in the mid-1890s in Chicago. Later owned by the Brunswick Corporation, the Studebaker Building was sold to Columbia College in 1983.

An early example of a glass curtain wall façade, the regional office and warehouse of the Studebaker Brothers Automobile Company Building designed by Solon S. Beman, today serves Columbia College as the Studebaker Building.

Commissioned by Lucius Fisher, a paper mogul, the Fisher Building, at 343 South Dearborn Street, standing eighteen stories and 275 feet high on the corner of West Van Buren, follows designs of Charles Atwood of D. H. Burnham & Co. Realized in 1895–96, it followed the Reliance as another virtuoso performance of Burnham's engineer, Edward C. Shankland. It surpassed the Reliance in speed of steel-frame construction, when its top thirteen and one-half stories were erected in fourteen days.

The foundation rests on 25-foot-long piles allowing for a footing pressure of 6,000 pounds per square foot, enough to easily support the building. At street level, the exterior composition of the Fisher Building is almost identical to the Reliance. Above, its endlessly repeated Gothic-inspired undercut, matt finished, speckled, orange, terra-cotta cast detailing lends the façade an illusionary depth, although it is actually as thin-skinned—complete with bays and stick-thin mullions—as the Reliance's glossy, creamy façade.

Opposite: The eclectic Fine Arts Building was once home to the Studebaker Automobile Company.

Above: The Fisher Building proved that terra-cotta was a cost-effective and decorative skin for a steel-framed building.

Left: The Fisher Building's top thirteen and one-half stories were erected in fourteen days, a world record in 1895.

A terra-cotta New-Gothic-inspired entrance to the Fisher Building.

The Fisher Building demonstrated that there seems to be no limit to terra-cotta ornamentation.

In 1906, a twenty-story addition, designed by Peter J. Weber, former associate of Burnham's, was added to its north side.

Like the Reliance before it, the Fisher proved steel construction to be quick and cost-effective especially when paired with a terra-cotta skin. It also proved that intricate ornament could be produced in multiple castings at a significant cost and time saving over hand- or even machine-carved stone.

The Chicago Building is one of three remaining buildings at an intersection that was once called the "busiest corner in the world." Built in 1904—5, on the southwest corner of Madison, it juts into State Street and since the successful campaign for

a uniform house numbering system in 1908 by Edward P. Brennan, is the 0-0 degree point for the city that marks the numerical center of Chicago from which all street addresses originate. Designed by Holabird & Root, the Chicago is a steel-framed structure that features large Chicago windows facing State Street and alternating with three banks of bays along Madison Street. It is also among the last buildings in the business district to have a dark terra-cotta skin. For the next couple of decades creamy glaze lightened terra-cotta and brightened the cityscape. In 1997, the School of the Art Institute acquired the building and converted it into a student dormitory.

In 1881, the Schlesinger & Mayer dry goods store moved into the Bowen Building, corner of Madison and State streets. Within a decade Adler & Sullivan were sought out to provide more space for the growing store. Proposals were made, none accepted. On July 1, 1895, Adler & Sullivan dissolved their partnership. Sullivan was retained by Schlesinger & Mayer and after several starts and changes of plans, the Madison portion was completed. Then in 1902 a twelve-story design was accepted. It is remarkable in its steel construction, spacing the supports to allow enormous display windows at ground level creating a sidewalk showcase bathed in daylight. Passers-by could see displays at eye level, mannequins dressed head to toe in the latest style.

On what was once the "busiest corner in the world," the Chicago Building is now the 0-0 numerical center for Chicago's uniform numbering system.

Above the ground floor, large composites composed of many 4x4 inch Luxfer prism glass tiles flooded the showrooms with natural light. Creamy white terra-cotta glowed from a distance. The steel framing allowed for light to flood in through large Chicago-style windows on the next eleven floors. Light allowed for each floor to optimize its goods, making them pleasing to the customer. Every floor was a point of sale. This was no office building.

Above left: Sullivan's Schlesinger & Mayer store was the aesthetic highpoint for Chicago's School of architecture.

Above right: Inspired by the look of Paris's department stores, Sullivan made its forms his own.

Sullivan achieved multi-story merchandizing. While a common merchandizing technique today, it was innovative then. With Schlesinger & Mayer he created a new way of selling goods.

At the corner of Madison and State Sullivan created a monumental cylindrical entrance that stood out; it could be seen from afar among all the other department stores vying for attention along State Street. Schlesinger & Mayer could not be missed. Also it was fireproof. The windows of the upper three floors retain the width of those below them, but not the height, reducing the visual blockness of the building. Along the uppermost floor a small recess supports a loggia topped by a highly detailed cornice that projects beyond the façade of the building, further reducing the visual block of the building.

In 1904 Carson Pirie Scott acquired the building. After the Christmas season of 2006 Carson's closed. After restoration of the interior and exterior, and a name change to the Sullivan Center, the School of the Art Institute of Chicago became a multi-floor tenant. After much speculation and more restoration, Target, a retailer, leased two floors in 2012.

Seen by many as one great advertisement of its product, the terra-cotta-clad Railway Exchange Building, standing on the northwest corner of Michigan and Jackson, was also corporate headquarters of the American Terra-cotta Co. The seventeen-story building was designed by Frederick P. Dinkelberg of D. H. Burnham and Co. and erected in 1903–04. Its creamy white terra-cotta façade and lobby are a distant reminder of the spectacular wealth of classical details available in terra-cotta without the need to rely on a specific classical vocabulary.

From across Michigan Avenue, the building is obviously a steel-frame structure with an undulating façade of projecting and recessing verticals of glass and terra-cotta reminiscent of the Burnham-designed Flatiron in Manhattan. Just below the hard cornice, oculi reference Sullivan's Wainwright in St. Louis and Guaranty in Buffalo. They soften the sudden transition of vertical surge to sky.

Having outgrown a cluster of smaller buildings, A. M. Rothschild & Co. commissioned Holabird & Roche in 1911 to design a new ten-story block-long department store at 333 S. State. A steel frame elegantly clad in creamy-yellowish terra-cotta with a proprietary "R" in a roundel, the building

Glazed creamy white, terra-cotta proves itself to be a worthy skin in an urban environment charged with soot.

Art Nouveau architectural ironwork does not get finer than on Carson's.

was a first-generation department store—conceived as a department store rather than developing into one like all the others had.

In 1936 the Rothschild Building became the flagship of the Chicago-based Goldblatt's chain and remained so until the mid-1980s. Purchased in 1993 by De Paul University as its Loop Campus, the store was converted into classrooms, offices and retail space, losing its north bay in the process. Inside, its College of Commerce, founded in 1912, the tenth accredited such school in the US, became the Driehaus College of Business in February 2012.

For a while after 1910, it appeared as if everything had been said and done, that height limits had sucked the boost out of Chicago, and all the city could do

Sullivan's ironwork helped Carson Pirie Scott department store become a worldwide architectural sensation.

The Railway Exchange Building, from 1904, shows Burnham's new direction with its white terra-cotta skin.

Chicago School architectural tradition slowly fades into classically inspired ornament in the Railway Exchange, while retaining its bay projections not unlike those of the 1880s.

was standardize the innovations of the 1890s. With Burnham turning his back on what had made him known, Sullivan receiving ever fewer commissions, others dying or retiring and single-family homes gaining attention and champions, the Chicago School of Architecture faded away in Chicago and the United States. Its influence blew across the Atlantic where it was strongly felt in Paris, Brussels, Vienna, Berlin, Amsterdam, Weimar, Dessau, Rotterdam, Brno, Haifa and Modernism everywhere, before it returned to Chicago and, in a different guise, again led the world of architecture.

Holabird & Roche
continue the
Chicago School's
department-store
tradition with the
Rothschild Building
from 1911.

With its
Renaissance-
inspired
ornamentation,
the terra-cotta
of the Rothschild
Store shines
towards the future.

PLACES TO VISIT

When you walk the streets of Chicago's downtown, you are in a museum of architecture. Guides are available in book or human form. The Chicago Architecture Foundation, located in the Railway Exchange Building, offers guided tours through the Loop and elsewhere. There are also several boat tours along the Chicago River and Lake Michigan. The Art Institute of Chicago has an Architecture Department and archive and there are architectural objects from Chicago buildings on permanent display. During the workweek most Loop buildings have lobbies that are accessible.

FURTHER READING

Blaser, Werner, ed. *Chicago Architecture: Holabird & Root, 1882–1992*. Basel: Birkhausen Verlag, 1992.

Condit, Carl W. *The Chicago School of Architecture: A History of Commercial and Public Building in the Chicago Area, 1875–1925*. Chicago: University of Chicago Press, 1964.

Cronon, William. *Nature's Metropolis: Chicago and the Great West*. New York: W. W. Norton, 1991.

Hoffmann, Donald. *The Architecture of John Wellborn Root*. Baltimore: John Hopkins University Press, 1973.

Mayer, Harold M. and Eichard C. Wade. *Chicago: Growth of a Metropolis*. Chicago: University of Chicago Press, 1969.

Pacyga, Dominic A. *Chicago: A Historical Guide to the Neighborhoods: The Loop and South Side*. Chicago: Chicago Historical Society, 1979.

Randall, Frank A. *The History of the Development of Building Construction in Chicago* (2nd ed., rev. and exp.). Urbana: University of Illinois Press, 1999.

Saliga, Pauline A. *The Sky's the Limit: A Century of Chicago Skyscrapers*. Reissued with additions, New York: Rizzoli, 1998.

Schulze, Franz and Kevin Harrington. *Chicago's Famous Buildings*, 4th rev. ed. Chicago: University of Chicago Press, 1993.

Sinkevitch, Alice, ed. *AIA Guide to Chicago*. 2nd Edition. Updated 2004. New York: A Harvest Original Harcourt, 2004.

Sullivan, Louis H. *The Autobiography of an Idea*. New York: Dover Books, 1964 reprint of 1924 original.

Zukowsky, John, ed. *Chicago Architecture, 1827–1922: Birth of a Metropolis*. Munich: Prestel Verlag, 1982.

INDEX

Page numbers in italics refer to illustrations

A. M. Rothschild & Co. 59,
60, *62*
Adler & Sullivan *3, 4*, 33,
34–8, *34, 35, 36, 37*, 38,
38, 57
Aldis, Owen 28, 29, 31–2
American Institute
of Architects 5
Atwood, Charles 40, 42, 55
Auditorium Building *3, 4*, 33,
34–8, *34, 35, 36, 37, 38*
Baumann, Frederick 14
Beman, Solon S. 53
Bogardus, James 11
Brewster Apartments 48, 50,
51, 52, 52
Brooks, Peter and Shepherd 29
Burnham & Root 7, 12, 21,
23, 25, 29, 36, 40, 42
Fisher Building 7, 21, 28,
29, 42
Burnham, Daniel 12, 21, 31,
32, 33, 38, 59, 61, *61*
Carson Pirie Scott *6*, 58, *58*,
59, *59*, 60
Chicago Building 57, *57*
Chicago Terra-cotta Co. 12
Chicago window 16
Construction of buildings 9
D. H. Burnham & Co. 55, 59
Dinkelberg, Frederick P. 59
Driehaus College of Business 60
Drummond, William 26
Eiffel, Gustave 15
Ellis, Peter Jr. 12
Fair Store *13*, 19, *19, 22*
Ferree, Barr 5
Ferris wheel *31*
Field, Marshall 15
Fine Arts Building 53, *54*
Fire: Great Chicago Fire of 1871:
10–1, *11*; of 1874: 13

fireproofing 13
First Leiter Building 15–6
Fisher Building 55, *55*, 56, *56*
Furness, Frank 34
Healy & Millet *35*, 36, *36*
37, 39
Holabird & Roche 39, 47, 48,
49, 59
Holabird & Root 57
Holzer, A. J. *45, 48*
Home Insurance Building
15, *15*, 16–7, *17*
Jenny, William Le Baron
14, 15–9, *15, 17, 18*,
19, 31, 40, *41*, 52
Johnson, George H. 12
Kendall Building 12
Lehmann, Ernst J. 19
Leiter, Levi 15
Loring, Sanford 12, 13
Manhattan Building 31, 40,
41, 42
Marquette Building *44, 46*,
47–8, *47*, 48
Masonic Temple 42, *43*, 45
McCutcheon, John T. *33*
McLaughlin, John 15
Mies van der Rohe, Ludwig
7, 40, 42
Monadnock Building 28–33,
28, 29, 30
Montauk Building 21
Old Colony Building 48,
49, 50
Paris 11, 15
Pittsburgh Plate Glass 47
Purdy, Corydon T. 47, 48
Railway Exchange Building
58–9, *61*
Reid House 42, *43*
Reliance Building *20*, 40,
41, *42*, 55–6
Rookery Building 12, 21–6,
22, 23, 24, 26, 27

Root, John Wellborn 12, 21,
31–3
Scagliola 36
Schlesinger & Mayer 57
Second Leiter Building 17, *18*
Seiffert, Carl 39
Shankland, Edward C. 40, 55
Shillito, John 15
Siegel, Cooper and Co. 18, *18*
Studebaker Building 53, *53*
Sullivan, Louis 5, 6, *6*, 7,
33, 34, *35*, 36, *36, 39,
50*, 57–8, *58*
Tacoma Building 39, *40*
Thomas, Theodore 37
Turnock, Enoch Hill 50, *52*
Van Osdel, John M. 12
Washington Block *8*, 14, *14*
Weber, Peter J. 56
Wight, Peter B. 13
Winslow Brothers 7
World's Columbian Exposition
31, *32*, 33, 50
Wright, Frank Lloyd 25–6